Table of Contents

Disclaimer

Think of me what you will, but the ideas exposed are what I believe to be the simple truths. The solutions are strategies that could get a whole lot of people out of the rat race and get this country moving forward in the right direction. I will tell you what I see happening and I will also tell you what you can do about what you see happening. I am not an attorney or a financial planner so you should check with a professional before you apply any of the steps outlined in this book.

Dedication

"Donald Sterling should not be asking what have our black celebrities done for the black community, black people should be asking what have they really done for the black community."
-J.Williams

I dedicate this project to all those who aspire to make their mark using their God-given abilities, for those who refuse to quit trying, for those who have the confidence to withstand the storm. To my mother who has always stood with me in the best and worst of times and to my wife Heather, and our daughter Michella Jae Williams. To Gary Spangler who gave me some great ideas and debated my theories until they were perfected.

It has been said that if you do not stand for something you will fall for anything. I would like to say if you do not live for something you will die for nothing. NEVER give up on your dreams and be fearless.

3

Introduction

In writing this book, I could have used a bunch of statistics, cited a bunch of references, and used some of the fancy charts as supporting documentation of the facts in this case. I will let the big publishing houses create those books which will certainly come in due time to line their pockets. I designed this book to be a quick read page-turner. So we will eat all the meat and leave the bones for the fact finders. Let me begin by saying that I stand with President Obama and many other educated Americans who say that what Donald Sterling said about black people is incredibly offensive and reflects the legacy of discrimination in America. Let me be clear: *I do not support the core values of Donald Sterling's racist remarks.*

However, the core message of this book is to underscore ideas, principles, and different theories of perception so that we can become a country who is not afraid to discuss race and the impact of race relations. It is my goal that the reader of this book will read it a second time objectively and discover lessons that will ultimately make us become a country of ambassadors setting the example for cultural diversity. Historical moments such as the recent Donald Sterling scandal occur very rarely and I hope to be an inspiration to others as those who were inspirational to me. You too can define your moment in history. I can remember those famous words by Harriet Tubman who said, "I've freed thousands of slaves and would have freed thousands more only if they knew they were slaves."

As Americans, we have a greater responsibility than ourselves and that is to each other and to our country. That responsibility involves strength, vigor, wholeness, wellness, and shape of humanity. After reading this if you feel the urge to go out there and start a movement then find the courage and voice your opinions. Can you uplift your spouse or offer a stranger some kind words and lend a helping hand, do whatever you can to pull somebody up. We should not live in a nation where we are peer pressured or mentally bullied to live through someone else's lens of reality. It is expected of you to show up and perform, no one should have to do what is expected of you to do. We all should seek to be fruitful in our endeavors. In a culture where so much value is placed on financial success, now is the time that our heads need to be in the game. As Booker T. Washington had said, "I have learned that success is to be measured not so much by the position that one has reached in life as by the obstacles which he has had to overcome while trying to succeed." Look at all the obstacles President Obama has had to overcome to get to where he is today. Stephen A. Smith is right when he talks about the American dream, he says not everybody can be Jay-Z or Beyonce; they are one in a billion. The American dreams is pulling yourself out of a bad environment, earning an education and legally have a means to support yourself even when the odds are stacked against you. Let us strive to improve our poor communities one at a time until we make this country the great nation that she has the potential to be.

The Truth about Magic Johnson

"Perhaps the Lord will see my affliction and restore goodness."

-King David

I believe Magic Johnson is a wonderful person, athlete, businessperson, and mentor. By no means do I have any kicks by expressing my point of views that are unfavorable to him and in no way am I taking away what contributions he has made. I do not know if you are familiar with his stats sheet but Magic's momma did not raise no punk. Magic's scorecard is just as impressive as Michael Jordan's is and more than Larry Bird's. Magic Johnson has been a champion for a very long time he even helped his team win the NCAA championship against Larry Bird way back in 1979. In fact, Magic Johnson has had just as many years in victory as Donald Sterling give or take a few rough days.

After college, Magic went on to have a very successful thirteen seasons with the LA. Lakers winning five championships and many other accomplishments too many to list.

However, for those of us who know the Bible, Magic Johnson's story is a story we are all too familiar with. Magic's story is a reflection of a biblical incident involving two literary characters name King David and Bathsheba but with a slight twist. King David and Magic possessed leadership qualities of character, charisma, charm, analytical thinking, and power. However, these same qualities caused David and Magic to do disastrous deeds, revealing that they are nothing but men perfectly flawed like everyone else. A leader is defined as "A person who leads a group of people, especially the head of a country or an organization." (Oxford English Dictionary). For a more in-depth definition, I like how Dr. Patterson and Dr. Winston describes a leader. "A leader is one or more people who selects, equips, trains, and influences one or more follower(s) who have diverse gifts, abilities, and skills and focuses the follower(s) to the organization's mission and objectives causing the follower(s) to willingly and enthusiastically expend spiritual, emotional, and physical energy in a concerted coordinated effort to achieve the organizational mission and objectives." (Winston, Patterson). It's pretty clear in retrospect from the fact sheet how Magic met the criteria to be a leader. How did King David fit the definition of a leader? From the very beginning, God sent Samuel to the house of Jesse in search for a new King saying, "I have chosen one of his sons to be king." (1 Samuel chapter 16). Also if we analyze the meaning of "David" which translates in Hebrew, Hebrew being the language of the Talmud, "daw-veed" means "beloved" or "chosen" (Slobin 342). David had God's favor because he was chosen by God himself to one day be King, he was predestined for a leadership position. "The glorious monarch who pushed the border of Israel to the fullest extent of God's biblical power." (Kirsch 105).

Unfortunately, all good things would come to an end and David, as "King", would fall victim to his own character flaws just as Magic Johnson. David had won the hearts and minds of both Israel and Judah because he had compassion for the people, like Magic had for those all around the world. The turning point for David's influence and loyalty was when his own acts of abuse of power had overtaken him. This is similar to Magic, who obtained fame, wealth, and acceptance from people in all walks of life. David's iconic demise started with an affair with a woman name Bathsheba, David was the King, he could have summoned any unmarried eligible woman at his discretion. Instead, he forces Bathsheba to sleep with him against her will, going against every principle and character that God had blessed him with and that the people had grown to love.

Magic had everything. He had achieve it all, he was a champion basketball player, he was a great role model, he gave us all hope and inspiration, he instilled in us the belief in ourselves, we trusted him and in return he gave us "Magic".

Then on that one frightening day in 1991 because of his abuse of power, he gave us that devastating announcement of the virus he had contracted as a result of sleeping with other women while married. Is this the kind of behavior that you would want your kids to conduct when they become young adults? Is this a good example of a role model? So when Donald Sterling asks what kind of man goes to every town in America and sleeps with every girl and contracts HIV, it is under THIS lens that he makes a valid point. This possession of power ultimately causes Magic to make poor choices and lose his loyalty amongst the people. When Magic has achieved real power, he sins, and God withdraws support from him. However, it is because Magic is not God but rather, a man, a human being with flaws and weaknesses that he fails. Magic, like King David had it all but instead of using his position to do well, he used it to betray trust at one point. Once he commits his heinous acts of betrayal, he squandered his blessings.

Therefore, just as he did to King David, God made Magic face the consequences.

Now as Magic has begun to continue rebuilding the bridges that he tore down we don't see the Magic he was, he had his wake up call posses the right heart condition and was given a second chance. It is because of Magic's journey that even more is expected from him. Magic Johnson is from Lansing MI, if you walk the streets of East Lansing and ask when was the last time they have seen Magic Johnson in the urban community offering apprenticeship programs, funding for black entrepreneurs, buying up the ghettos you'll be real disappointed. It's not always about money. Magic Johnson could use his sway, his investors, his words of influence politically, and his name to open doors. Perhaps Magic could of collaborated with the Detroit

Pistons, Redwings, Detroit Lions football players and saved Detroit. Where is the voice of Magic Johnson at the White House working on cultural changes, fighting to end the war on poverty a.k.a The Drug War, joining the hands of Bill Cosby in the attempt to uplift the moral of the minority community? He has the potential to be the next Dr. Martin Luther King but maybe I'm wrong.

Jews vs. Blacks

"Liberty cannot be preserved without general knowledge amongst the people."-John Adams

Donald Sterling said that it "appears that when Blacks make it they don't want to help anybody out." First of all he is entitled to have whatever perception of what black people appear to be doing in his eyes. It's his opinion right or wrong, he's 82 years old and any man is entitled to speak his mind. My mother will tell you in a heartbeat what is in her head whether you like the way she put it or not but usually she is right. I coined the term "speaking in blunts" because she is so blunt about everything. I can remember asking her if she had any care or concern as to how her words make other people feel and she said, " I'm too old to beat around the bush might as well get straight to the point." She went on to say at her age every minute wasted is like a year off her life and you know what, she is right. If you consider the people you are speaking with as grown folk, why not be more candid? It leads to a more healthier and meaningful discussion. If my breath stinks and it is offensive then you should offer me a breath mint so we can get past that and bear fruit from the discussion.

What makes matters worst is Donald Sterling is right - black people need to stop being so sensitive. Donald said "What does he do?" and here we can lay out Magic Johnson's laundry list of contributions. Then Donald asks, "I mean big Magic Johnson, what does he really do?" It is at this point you get the value of what he is bringing to the conversation. What he is really asking is for the black community to look around. What impact has he made in your 'hood by changing a broken system that is in favor of suppressing black people. He has sent millions to help HIV awareness, great! He sent 150 people off to college, great! He is a successful business owner that employs black people, great! All that is great but it is the equivalent of a father out on a business trip on his son's birthday but he sends a gift in the mail. What Magic has done an average man with 30 million dollars can do. As of this writing, Magic has an estimated 700 million dollar net worth, a plethora of great business ventures, partners, artist friends, and entertainers in pop culture. And it is a sad day in hell when Tupac Shakur has done more politically for black people in the 'hood in death than Magic Johnson and Tyler Perry has done alive. This is the perception Donald Sterling has when he made those comments because when you look at things in the broader scope Magic has done very little.

Millions of young black men get trapped into the drug war every year. (I recommend reading "The New Jim Crow" by Michelle Alexander.) There is still countless numbers of individuals of the black race still homeless, unemployed and underinsured. This is no means to say that all the burden should fall on Magic's shoulders, but once he earned the title as ambassador of peace, Magic describes himself as a leader of the black community and yes, he has earn a stature that we all aspire to but go to the prisons and ask when was the last time they've seen Magic.

The thing is, Magic doesn't have to use his money. He could use his charm, charisma and wit to influence many other powerful men who control the keys to opportunity. He could further the efforts of other black community leaders and business development centers. I'm from Flint

MI. and I have never heard of Magic Johnson coming here to do anything. In fact he started a youth center in Saginaw which is about 30 minutes from Flint and my mom wrote him a letter to start one in Flint MI. No one from Magic's organization ever responded. I go to the S.B.A. which is barely government funded and offer mediocre services consisting of a bunch of brochures on programs not available to our district.

The most valuable nugget of information that came out of that interview was when Donald Sterling stated, "The Jewish people have a company and it's for people who want to borrow money at no interest," Sterling says. "We want to help people. If you don't have money, we'll loan it to you. If you don't have interest [sic], one day you'll pay us back. I'm just telling you—he (Magic) does nothing. It's all talk." That is the part where the black community should be centered on, the racist part will obviously take care of itself. This man should be honored for giving us this key to success and that is helping each other - think about it, the Jews do it, the Saudis do it, the Chinese do it, Chaldeans do it, why don't black people do it? Pay attention to how these other ethnicities comes to America and prosper within five years and you'll realize that backing each other is their secret formula. If Donald Sterling gets thrown out of the NBA for anything it is going to be not what he said about black people, but the fact that he pointed out our weakness. It may have upset a lot of Jewish people because Jewish people move in silence, he not only discussed the principle of Jewish law but he shared it with the whole wide world. He gave the world the key to life or death for any culture: to have self dependence. They don't teach that in college and for that he may pay a price.

Here is an analogy, if you and I were friendly opponents in a weekly basketball tournament in the neighborhood and during our games I pointed out you can't drive to your left, you need to work on that. Before finals time you're going to strengthen those weaknesses until it become as good as your strengths. That is essentially what Donald Sterling did when he made that comment. He saw that we as black people don't have a banking system in place or a lending option where we can't be marginalize by white people so we will never initiate real change. Frankly, I was embarrassed as a black man after I thought about what he said. If we don't change business growth and development amongst our own people will forever fall behind and no amount of money in the world would matter because we didn't teach our black people how to fish, we never gave them a fishing pole we only fed them fish. For this insightful observation Donald Sterling should receive a lifetime achievement award because he revealed the root of the plague for the black race. Black people are wealthy enough, powerful enough to the point where we don't have to look to government, or quicken loans to finance our dreams and secure the outcome of our retirement. Look what happened when we depended on Delphi and GM. Why aren't we as black people holding these rich black people who are out here wasting millions of dollars on needless consumer goods accountable? Bill Cosby has been trying to address this for years. If black leaders really wanted to initiate an effective campaign to bring about the change that is eroding the minds of our young people then we should not be avoiding this discussion at the round table. Let's put a spot light on the amount of money blacks waste in strip clubs, jewelry, cars, clothes, and designer shoes. Black people creating slaves to clothing labels and car manufactures without even thinking about it. Correcting this mismanagement of funds could turn criminals into legitimate entrepreneurs.

I often hear people say that "if we do something as you suggest, it would be discriminating against whites", but not when you make it a part of a program or grant geared towards urban development. Whites have their own programs, so do the Jews, and Chaldeans. I've seen in past history the kind of programs Magic has funded for urban development and what happens is the money for construction go towards the white construction companies.

The sad truth is that since the recession many of the construction companies hire very few blacks and the corporate politics prevent minorities from reaching their full potential within the company. Also there is favoritism in what is supposed to be a blind bid whereas a black company may submit a lower bid but do not get the contract for the big projects like the urban development projects at Magic's 16 centers. So what Donald Sterling is asking, is how many minority businesses have Magic and other celebs such as Michael Jordan, Oprah, Denzel Washington, Morgan Freeman, etc. funded that has change the course of the black community? Think about it!

Blacks and Politics

"There is a moral [and] constitutional equivalence between laws designed to subjugate a race and those that distribute benefits on the basis of race in order to foster some current notion of equality. Government cannot make us equal." - Clarence Thomas

Think of the celebrity musicians, actors, athletes, authors, talk show hosts, and everyone else who has benefited from Dr. Martin Luther King, Marcus Garvey, Arthur Ashe, Harry Bellefonte, Dr. Dyson, Cornell West and countless other contributors. Now measure that against the rich black people today who have more money, less barriers, and technology all to their advantage the impact their making pales in comparison. Those past black leaders made real sacrifices for a better tomorrow; it was far a cry from donating money to avoid higher taxes, or using celebrity status to donate other people's money. Any celebrity can donate an hour to give a youth group some mentorship, or play a sport to raise charity. When question why only an hour of their time it's always the same answer, " Do you know how much I make an hour?" It's pretty selfish when you think about it.   Perhaps we should track all their expenses that they waste that could be use to help in politics, change lives and cut down the recidivism, rebuild ghettos, after all they have a responsibility to the minority community and based on what we have seen, we can't forget that.

In Myrtle Beach every year in a prominent downtown area they have what's called biker week and typically Harley Davidson week arrive first in town and thousands of bikers from all over come together to party, hang out in the bars spending a ton of money. It's good for local businesses.

Around one week later it's black bikers week and typically during this period more police are called to the city to police the wild drunk disorderliness, bike races, loud music, open sex, and vandalism. Afterward when they're gone the city has so much trash left behind it take the city workers three times longer to clean than the Harley week. It has gotten so bad that when black biker week comes around some of local businesses close down because they lose money. In fact at the time of this writing, three days ago three people got killed during black bikers week in a town that typically doesn't have any violent crime. This is why we get a bad reputation because our people are displaying this kind of conduct.

To facilitate change maybe we need a Black Monetary Fund (B.M.F.) that provides funding for Political Action

Committees (P.A.C.'s) that tackle corruption in the grants being handed out from the Federal government such as funding being given to revitalize those underdeveloped projects but is being stolen in the form of huge salaries for the controlling officers. Or the contract favorites who disperse a kick back behind closed doors, look at Kwame Kilpatrick for example. It is sad when most of our political pull comes from underground artist like Mos Def, Professor Griff and ZaZa Ali, who speak about the times of today the struggle in the black community. However because they're not mainstream they have to work four times as hard to get the message in front of a larger audience. When was the last time you seen T.D. Jakes, Tiger Woods, Michael Jordan, Collin Powell, Condoleezaa Rice, on their soap box. They have enough money and political pull that they could really get things done if they wanted to and yet where is the change?

We as a people can't turn a blind eye to the injustices, inequalities, lack of representation, in the black community. In fact many rich black people have shown us that they all agree with Justice Clarence Thomas who thinks that the best way to deal with race in America is to not talk about it or to say that "Americans today are too sensitive about race" to have a meaningful discussion. And now, Donald Sterling has open that door.

This Black Monetary Fund should hold monthly press conference addressing us nationally about the progress they are making as a collective whole. There should be one common goal, not these individual agendas by individual people. There should be one government body that have many branches of lower level government that deals with different agendas like banking, medicine, bioengineer, computer programming, sciences, education, etc. that way the money will draw more interest. This could be the next big government that have an agenda to work with the federal government to rebuild Detroit, Chicago, St. Louis, and other troubled cities one at a time. Can you imagine at what rate of speed this county would move forward? Everyone of these celebs or rich black people listed in this book have started their own charity of some own personal cause and that is great, it's better than doing nothing but what I'm saying is we need to work smarter. Just stop and think about the amount of money it takes for lawyers, government filing fees, and expenses to start every single charity, now multiply this number by the number of black millionaires who have started their own charities. That expense alone would probably be a billion in savings.

After understanding all this think about the impact of this Donald Sterling incident and ask yourself, has he done more than Michael Jordan, Tiger Woods, Collin Powell and a long list of others? Quite frankly Donald Sterling has now opened the door to start a movement in the right direction. I have never heard of a team of celebrities traveling to a troubled city, meet with city officials and ask what can they do collectively to get this city back on track. Instead of anger, that should be one of the take aways from Donald Sterling's remarks.

Donald's Performance Track

"If we don't make earnest moves towards real solutions then every day we move one more day closer to revolution and anarchy in this country."-Louis Farrakhan

Donald has employed more black people than any black business I can think of over his 35 year tenure including B.E.T. the Black Entertainment Network. What happens in his personal life didn't affect his performance on the job in fact Donald has a stellar track record and should be commended for the value he has added to the L.A. Clippers since his time of purchase. It took him a while and he may of had the worst season record, but in business we all don't become successful overnight, there's always a learning curve. What matters most is where he is today. He took the risk, made the sacrifice, and weathered the storm when bringing the LA Clippers to LA. This move happened to be a huge benefit to the NBA league, the players, and

himself. You have to reward genius after all; we are a
country of good ideas.

Donald Sterling is the all-American success story; he is a
gold mine of knowledge and experience. The NBA and the
black community missed an opportunity to forcibly tap into
that genius with their decision to outcast him. They should
of given him a dollar amount fine and considered making
him participate in some apprenticeship program where you
take so many teams of 12 people, men and women, that
would be allowed to work under him and learn the ins and
outs of running a successful business. He could teach them
how to market, how to manage, real-estate strategies,
canvassing for land to develop, how to do corporate
planning, learning tax strategies, how to run charities, and
so much more for as long as he owned the team. This is a

guy who bought a team at 12.5 million dollars and turned it into what some speculate to now be a billion plus dollars. That doesn't happen by accident.

Donald Sterling is the longest owner in the NBA. He has employed a significant number of black people and yes, by being employed they are able to put food on their table, clothes on the kid's back, and provide funding for tuitions. Donald is the son of immigrant parents who came to America to live the American dream and faced his share of stereotypes, racism, and broke down financial roadblocks because of his Jewish blood. Similar to the black struggle Donald did what blacks should do and that is earn an education, develop a skill, and go into business for yourself. Those are things that no one can take from you. Donald had the education and the chutzpah to overcome adversity that he inherited from his parent's teachings, things that black mothers and fathers need to be providing for their children. Donald refused to quit, he believed in himself. He is a fighter and has fought his whole life like Floyd Mayweather, which is what made Donald a champion.

For a guy who doesn't like black people did you know that he has signed the biggest contract in franchise history to a black player name Elden Brand for 82 million dollars? Go ask Elden if he thinks Donald is a racist. People have questioned the authenticity of Donald's service to the black community and I take issue with that. Donald learns the importance of being a good servant at his father's small produce store where he worked as a grocer bagger in one of the poorest areas of Los Angeles. His parents put away every penny and lived below their means, not above their means to send Donald to a good University because they knew the value of an education. Donald worked late hours to pitch in what he could by taking on part time work at an furniture store. He developed customer service and retail skills but most important a good work ethic. Donald knows what it is like to be discriminated against. He even decided to change his name and image to fit in the norms of society and break the threshold of resistance. What are black people in the urban community doing to change their image?

One of the problems of black people today is that they want society to conform to a lower standard by accepting laziness, broken English, sagging pants, speaking derogatory language, and their hair all over the place. Black people today are doing all this loud talking, disrespecting each other, posting pictures on Facebook with guns and drugs, we got women who are posing half naked and humiliating themselves. It is to the point where because of all this we don't have to worry about corporate America passing us over for a position because we eliminate ourselves. You might say that white people do the same thing, well white people own their own businesses too. At a time when the economy is recovering from a financial down turn and employment is scarce and a large percentage of minorities are still unemployed, you would think our level of professionalism would be at an all time high. But we as black people quit too easy and prefer to join others who blame the white man for all our problems. As a black man who grew up in the urban community I know we might not be able to change our skin color but we can learn to speak proper English, act civilized, and carry ourselves in a way other races will see us and know that we demand to be respected. Look how good the brothers from the Nation of Islam have branded themselves and everybody knows they are serious and command respect. Bill Cosby has been working on encouraging us to assume responsibility for ourselves so that we can begin to change the way others perceive us for years.

Donald Sterling's performance track speaks volumes and should inspire us all not to quit because success may be right around the corner. He says he has personally tried over 10,000 cases in the court of law, now that's tenacity! Most of the problems with blacks who could be entrepreneurs is that they quit too easy. I say "you got to be hungry" in (my Les Brown voice). Donald used his education, savings, connections, and entrepreneurial spirit to win and win big. That is the page I'm looking to take from his book of life. Before this incident many of us didn't know who he was. Look at his long list of charitable donations on Citizenaudit.org just dating back to 2008. It's a lot of money and this is a guy who has been contributing to society and black people before 1981. If you added up all his donations include inflation and the impact on causes as a result of his donations, in my opinion, he has done more for black people than Michael Jordan, especially in light of his recent interview with Anderson Cooper. This interview has so much value because he let out some really good information and highlighted areas of weakness for the black community so that we can begin to move forward in the right direction. I don't know what Michael Jordan does secretly as far as politics but never in my life time have I seen him voice his position on issues striking the black community. Where is Jordan on his soap box? Jordan has the potential to have so much more positive influence on the minds of some of the most troubled youth who purchase his $200 sneakers.

Furthermore, Donald Sterling has been a family member to the NBA and for the league to represent a brotherhood; you can't turn your back on your brother when he has succumbed to such illness. "We are not just a league office, we are not just a league of players, we are collectively one family." - Kevin Johnson.

Why Donald Sterling's Contributions are "Fair Game"

"Religion without humanity is very poor human stuff."

-Sojourner Truth

I stand with Andy Roser in the belief that what was said on that tape doesn't reflect the heart of who Donald Sterling is and his other black supporters should speak up. The NAACP and the UCLA should have not felt compelled by political pressure to giving their charitable contributions back in this time of economic recession. The fact that they do not share his core values is fine but this is a setback to the overall mission and promised recipients of the charity. If I'm a kid with cancer expecting chemotherapy from funding that Donald Sterling contributed do you think it is fair that I would suffer until we find replacement funding? Of course not, that's nonsense. That money serves the community in some cases, minorities. By not accepting the funding is counterproductive to uplifting humanity. If I may use an analogy, that is like saying "let's tear down Miami because it was built with money from the cocaine cowboys", or "let's tear down Las Vegas and rebuild it because it was built by the mafia". Have you ever heard of the FBI or DEA burning money, destroying luxury houses, cars, and jewelry because it was owned by drug dealers? I'm quite sure they don't share the same values as the drug dealers but you don't hear about them giving those things back.

I have never heard of the FBI or DEA returning seized money or proceeds from forfeitures to the neighborhoods that they seized them from, either. They could call it grant money and rebuild the same run down ghettos, and build youth clubs, business centers, and address teen pregnancy. These kinds of ideas would initiate the kind of nucleus that would forever change so many lives of the urban community. That is why the NAACP and UCLA should never ever cave into political pressure because no one offered to replace the donation until the public weighed in. Charities have missions a lot greater than Donald Sterling and deserve to be carried out with purpose and be bulletproof from the rhetoric. The NAACP and the UCLA or any other charity should stick to its mission by solving problems, not creating them. Now without Mr. Sterling UCLA has created a 3 million dollar headache. I didn't hear Magic say that he'll cover that from his charity nor did any of the other black NBA players. More importantly, you can't define someone a racist on one end of the spectrum and then on the other end win awards for charitable given to minorities, which is an oxymoron at its best.

In a Forbes article titled, "The Truth about Charity", Given Sheds touches on four points that is relevant to this story. It is not uncommon for celebrities to promote their image through charities, so Donald Sterling is not the first one to do that. The biggest one he discovered is that celebrities create charities to provide relatives work, but Donald Sterling runs his charity himself. Look at his 2012 990-tax form when compared side by side to Magic and his charities, Donald Sterling happens to run his own charities more efficiently than Magic, and that is even after Magic pays his controller of the charity 7% of the contributions. Also it is common practice for big name celebrities to lend their celebrity names and status to raise donations without possibly giving any money of their own. However, I think Donald Sterling is a straight shooter because he contributes money right out of his pocket for the last 35 years and 15 to 25 years with the NAACP.

Fruit from the Poisonous Tree

The Donald Sterling debacle is a true miscarriage of justice. I agree that Donald Sterling's poor choice of words and mischaracterization was offensive and damaging to himself and to black America. However, in reality I honestly do not think in his heart he meant it the way it came out on the recording, let me explain. In the 'hood when my friends and I went on a car ride to try to holler at girls, often times these girls would be out walking and we would ride up on them. We were horny young boys and we would say anything I mean anything to get these girls to get in the car with us. At the time I was 16 years old I can remember vividly a girl once said, "I got a man." We would say something like, "Okay well he a loser" and she said, "My man is not a loser he has a job". We would say, "Oh yea where at?" She said, "Wal-Mart". We started dying laughing, we made fun of his job, putting him down, flashing our money and brash ways from running the street thinking that we were better off. Ironically, we had no clue how important him having a job would play out until many years later when we learned that you need credit, proof of income to buy new cars, or a house, and get bank loan approvals to finance your dreams.

What a slap in the face, the joke was on us because that kid had several years of seniority at a well-established company, benefits, and good work history. My point is when Donald Sterling was talking to "V" he was running game on her and at 82 yrs old you may say you saw God part the sky to have sex with a young attractive woman like her let's keep it real.

If you listen to the tape he had no bones with Magic, in the beginning he said he don't want to receive calls from his friends reporting back to him that she was hanging out with black guys, particularly "Magic Johnson". Let me translate this to you in pimpology: his friends are trying to warn him that "you may want to get a blood test before you run up in that again. I seen "V" hanging out with Magic and you know he has a history of being a ladies' man in the past. He has cheated on Cookie before so don't take any chances." Now at this instant put yourself in Donald's shoes, he has feelings for this girl, he has invested time, money, and emotions so you can understand how he could be angered. He was hurt bad, she played him; it was in the heat of passion that he made those comments because the black man made him inferior. I don't think he had a slave mentality when he said "I support them and give them food, and clothes, and cars, and houses. Who gives it to them? Does someone else give it to them? I know that I have -- Who makes the game? Do I make the game, or do they make the game?" In pimpology, Donald was trying to explain to a very simple girl that he was the big kahuna, that he is the one writing the checks, or other words "why would you choose to screw the help when you got me?" I get that, go back and listen to the tape objectively because later he says, "You think I'm a racist." Why would he ask her that question after everything he just said? Beside I seen a lot of racist people and most of them use the n-word. The part about the way blacks are treated in Jerusalem is not the product of his doing but we should thank him for exposing light on a belief system that resonated within the Jewish community in this country and around the world.

Black Monetary Fund (B.M.F.)

If a free society cannot help the many who are poor, it cannot save the few who are rich. - J.F.K.

Donald Sterling is right because many of these rich black people got rich off the purchasing power of the minority community, the same community Magic sold out to Howard Schultz in that Starbucks deal. He must of told Howard "they will become great employees, they will take the shirt off their back for you." And guess what they did. Had the conversation went like "they will be great employers" it never would of happen. Perhaps one idea is to form a consortium that acts as the black IRS that puts a spotlight on these under developed neighborhood projects and weigh in on who gets what out of it. After branding Starbucks as a black own franchisee he later sold it back to

Howard quietly for a nice profit but we didn't hear that part. One of the things the black community lack is a real effort to hold those accountable who have the platform to convert the mindset of those lost looking for leadership. Many black athletes, entertainers, actors, and preachers, title themselves as leaders of the black community; they have tons of charities but the fact of the matter is how are black people really doing? The black community has the kind of problem you can't just throw money at. You hear black people saying things like, "When is Obama going to do something for us?" My question is when are you going to do something for Obama? John F. Kennedy put it best, "Ask not what your country can do for you — ask what you can do for your country."

Most of the black charities today provide real contributions to the community and uplift humanity on the surface but let's examine the fruits of their labor in more detail. Consider the pay scale of highly paid rich black people and contrast that with the percentage they donate to charity. Most of those numbers are very disappointing. It is no secret that one way for these higher pay scale people to reduce their tax burden is to donate to charity. It is a simple tax planning strategy that requires no effort. What about these charities geared towards causes such as education, chronic disease, HIV, and others build field houses, museums, youth centers, and revitalize underdeveloped inner cities aren't they real?

What is the back-story to what really happens in some cases like scholarships for college education for minorities?

What is the percentage of students that graduate? What field of study are they pursuing? How many upon graduation walk into a position with a company? How many, after obtaining experience, start their own company? Is there further support along the way? How many reach back and help someone else get out of the struggle? These questions need to be under close scrutiny and answered so that stride of success and those charity dollars can go one-step further.

Let us take another look at the number of contributions and the amount of money that minorities have contributed for medicine. How many of those same black people own the intellectual property to any of the vaccines or other bioengineering like Bill Gates? Have you recently heard of a black-owned hospital that hired minority doctors to develop real progress in medicine that won't compromise or yield to politics and big pharma? If you put a dream team together like Oprah, Bob Johnson, Magic Johnson, Dick Parsons, etc. they could build the next John Hopkins. Here is my point, In Chicago alone Oprah, Michael Jordan, Kanye West, Quincy Jones, Terrance Howard, Common Sense, Robert Townsend, just to name a few, can merge that talent meet with preachers, community organizers, politicians, and city officials, and begin to write a new script for the city of Chicago. Let's lean on those business relationships, lean on their celebrity influence with these impressible minds and stop the bloodshed.

Starting one city at a time black people themselves can bring about the change to end the black plight. When you evaluate the facts there is no excuse for Chicago to be the ways it is, with the money they blow on campaigning it would be enough tear down and rebuild the ghetto. By giving Chicago's construction economy a boost and give minorities a set of career skills, this will boost morale, and put a dent in poverty. Let us start now changing what white America thinks about black people. That is why even after Oprah's 43 year career tenure and all the money, fame, and respect she has acquired she was told she couldn't afford that purse because her skin was still black. What happens in Chicago is a reflection of what people from around the world think about black people. You can't blame them, but you can change them.

Everyone will tell you money will not buy you happiness, money is a tool, so then why are black people refusing to use their tools to fix their problems? That is a missed opportunity. At the time of this writing the best interest return my bank can promise is 6% yield. What is 6% ROI when a small portion of your entire net worth could secure the outcome of a promising future? The bible say's let us be fruitful and multiply? What it is saying to other ethnicities is that black people don't have the confidence to invest in each other why should we invest in them; it is better kept under the mattress. Let us change the course of American history and start moving forward in the right direction today.

So Donald Sterling is right when he states it was his opinion that it seems that "blacks when they make it they don't want to help each other". Black people need to be honest you don't have to go far, just log in to Facebook. I see it all the time where blacks complain that black people don't ever want to help each other out. Why get mad when Donald Sterling say it? There is two types of classes within the black community that discriminate against each other. One type is the conservative blacks who wear their pants around their waist, and then there are the thugs who don't. People ask me was I emotionally charged by the racist remarks that Donald Sterling made and I said no because I hear black people calling each other far worse every day.

Again, it is a sad day in hell when Tupac has done more for the black people politically in death than Michael Jordan, Magic Johnson, Oprah, Tiger Woods, and Bob Johnson, and that is because Tupac's words touched everybody.

"In What Instances is Discrimination Fair Game"

"Other people's opinion of you does not have to become your reality." -Les Brown

Discrimination in many instances is fair game, for example, my mother live in Flint, MI and she has a Kroger grocery store 5 minutes from her house but she drives 20 minutes away from her house to a Kroger across town to buy her groceries. She has done this over the last 10 years and it is not because she is out enjoying a scenic view. When asked why, this is how she puts it, "When you pull into the parking lot of the Kroger 5 minutes from my house, black people are parked all outside the lines, loud rap music, you see black men with their pants falling off their behind where you can see their underwear, and I always walk in somebody's gum that they have spit out on to the ground.

The women are strutting around half naked trying to control some kid who is bumping into everyone else's shopping cart." This is an instance where discrimination is fair game. Everyone is entitled to their own peace of mind, I got an uncle who I love to death but he drinks too much. His clothes are always engulfed with the smell of alcohol so when he asks for a ride I tell him I can't do it; this is an instance where discrimination is fair game.

I'm black and as Mark Cuban said, if I see a black man walking down the same street as me and he has a black hoodie on I will walk across the street and not so much the same for a bald headed white guy with tattoos. Why? Because typically where I'm from more people who are my color have done harm to me than white people. Furthermore, I don't have experiences of bald headed white guys covered in tattoos robbing black people. What I have experienced them doing is robbing banks and usually that comes from what I see on the news or in the movies. However, if the black hoodie had UCLA or Shaq on the front I probably wouldn't feel threaten. Therefore, in these instances discrimination is fair game. This stereotype is not the blame of the individuals perception of reality, it lies with the way black people carry themselves, the role they play in movies, in videos, and it is this depiction that's hard to overcome when in real life and the movies appear to be so "real".

It is the job of the black community to change the perception of the way others see them. Black people can begin educating the youth about the power of perception early in the home. It is hard for the black child to see the problem with the black hoodie when he walks out the door and the kid across the street is wearing one also. It is the parents job and the neighboring community to educate their children about choosing clothing the will be perceived in their best interest. That is the culture and like Donald Sterling said, "It's too big to change."

It was reported that Donald Sterling didn't want to rent to black people and at the time the story broke no one took a head count of all his properties and reported back that he had zero black people as tenants. If they were able to prove this then that would have been good grounds for discrimination. If he had a bad tenant that gave him a poor perception of a certain kind of tenant then as an investor, he should protect his investment that is fair game. Public opinion can't dictate what's best for business or choose a planning strategy that would diminish the value of an investment because of politics.

If Elgin Baylor felt as he did about Donald Sterling, can you explain to me why someone as smart as Elgin would dedicate 22 yrs of his life working for this man? Donald must have treated him good until they had a disagreement and then just as "V" Stiviano tried, Elgin tried to burn him too. Do you think Doc Rivers, another honorable, respectable guy would work for Donald if he had witnessed these offenses that Donald has been accused of? No. Furthermore, Donald Sterling showed no signs of racism to the current L.A. Clippers team and what happened was illegally recorded outside the work place. Can you imagine if the shoe was on the other foot, everyone in the black community would be crying foul. In this case discrimination against Donald Sterling is not fair game, he is the victim here. That's right, Donald Sterling is the victim. His right of privacy was violated and the N.B.A has taken unfair action against him on the premise of "fruit from the poisonous tree." How come Louis Farrakhan can stand on his soapbox and say white man this, white man that, devil this, devil that, and where are all the leaders of the black community to defend their white friends that are not racist? Racial equality is for everyone and can lead to meaningful progress. My dad taught me that I put my pants on one leg at a time just like everybody else.

Are his words hurtful? Yes. Slave master rooted? Yes. Unhealthy rhetoric to spread? Yes, but there is far worse language being used everyday by black people to each other and that is what's so disturbing. Donald is right when he said the owners make the game, it's their marketing, branding, ingenuity, and business acumen that has caused the value of the NBA league and its players to rise. Not the players because even to this day there is still not one team who could play like the Bulls with Michael Jordan, Magic Johnson and the Lakers, Larry Bird and the Celtics, the Twin Towers in San Antonio etc., but that last part is my opinion. As a kid I tried to tell my parents how to run their house and that didn't go to well.

Why am I writing this?

"A change is brought about because ordinary people do
extraordinary things."
— Barack Obama

I can withstand the burden of risk. I don't have anything to

lose and chances are Oprah, Magic, Jordan, Bob Johnson,

and the list goes on won't be financing my business, rather

it will be more like Victoria from my Flagstar bank up the

street. More importantly, I'm writing this because I was

inspired by what Stephen A. Smith of ESPN when he said

speak up regardless of what the backlash may be.

Regardless if people call you porch monkey, honkey lover,

or Uncle Tom, frankly I've been called a helluva lot worst

usually by some black person. What good is it to attack

Donald Sterling and lay 400 years of frustration at his feet?

I think that once the ball started rolling with the help of the media it persuaded those sponsors to withdraw support, the young players, the commissioner, and the other owners.

I'm writing this because I know firsthand what it feels like to be railroaded, labeled as something you're not. In fact, what happened to Donald Sterling is exactly what happens to black people everyday in courtrooms all across America, how ironic. I'm not writing this to replace the words that were spoken. His words were very offensive but in America it is not illegal, what is illegal is the violation of right of privacy. Therefore, any action taken by the Commissioner and the members of the league regardless of the NBA constitution would be unconstitutional in the court of law and the ruling would be overturned effective immediately. We have an American constitution that takes precedent over any other formal or writing agreement between two people or organizations. For example, in real estate I can't force you to a binding contract for a lease if I never received a certificate of occupancy because legally even though the agreement between both parties is in good faith, it would be an illegal contract.

Donald Sterling was illegally removed from his position and he was correct in his actions to sue the NBA in these proceedings. Even at 82 his mind is still sharp and punctual, he had the NBA by the gonads and from the pressure surrounding the scandal or likelihood of diminishing the value of his investment, he resisted the opportunity to try this case. For the record, I don't think Donald Sterling's heart stand behind the words he used on that tape, he added the negative connation to underscore that he was the boss, he was above it all.

The most important reason I'm writing this is to turn our attention towards our black Celebrities, Athletes, Actors, Preachers, Musicians, etc. with all this power, money, and talent so that we can develop a real agenda for the black community. Through banking, politics, business, and so much more we can create great black employers instead of great black employees. Where is the figurehead for the next Million-Man March? We all know Jay-Z, Oprah, Michael Jordan, Magic Johnson, Lebron James can all draw a crowd because they sell out every arena. How come that much planning doesn't go into building our black community? That alone is "Why Donald Sterling is Right."

Conclusion

This story will come and go, and what will happen is nothing will come out of this historic event. Everyone will go on with his or her daily routine, sitting, waiting around until the next recording come out. This book should be seen as a guide giving direction on where to go from here, the blueprint to creating a plan of action. I'm not suggesting that inside you'll find all the answers because things are always changing and to be relevant you must change with the times. What I do know is this was or is a perfect opportunity to use Donald Sterling to begin changing the way Jewish people treat Blacks, and the way Blacks treat Blacks. It is this culture he spoke of that is the quiet killer, spreading hate in silence, a bunch of wolves in sheep's clothing and who knows, they could of been disguised as

C.E.O.'s of corporations, banks, politicians, or even sitting next to Donald at the owners club. You can be sure that by getting caught he pissed a bunch of Jewish people off because he revealed secrets strategies to build wealth, and the general public heard it all.

It is too bad that the black community was in such a rush to release those 400 years of frustration on Donald that they over looked the key points in the tape. Donald Sterling is a Jewel with a treasure trove of knowledge, can you imagine having the opportunity to pick his brain. However, we will never know what we could of known, what we need to know, to help move this country forward faster. Can you imagine 35 years or more of life's work and experience being summed up in a 15-minute phone call? Ouch.

The End

Work Cited

Kirsch Jonanthan. *The Five Books of Moses. Print.*

Slobin Dan. The Cross-linguistic Study of Language Acquisition.*Print.*

Winston. Patterson Ph.D. *An Integrative Definition of Leadership:* 2005